PREFACE TO BOOK VI

Keys and key signatures.—For a discussion of these matters see Prefaces to Books I, II, and III.

SOLFA TRAINING

It is assumed that solfa training has been sound, and is being continued. To attempt to apply solfa names to the staff without thorough and systematic modulator practice previously is to court disaster. Reading to laa is usually mere guess-work. No certainty can be obtained without a constant use of the solfa syllables. If a good foundation of solfa has been laid most easy leaps are prepared for. Reading from solfa notation also is an indispensable aid to securing fluency in the use of the syllables. Material for this will be found in Books XI and XII, which contain solfa notation only: they are intended to be preparatory and complementary to the staff books.

GRADING

No collection of sight-singing examples can possibly meet all needs, or suit everybody's plan of grading. To secure sufficient variety, and to maintain interest in class, it is necessary to employ various forms of reading practice by use of the modulator, written examples and printed tests. Teachers should be ready to invent, and write on the board, additional melodies giving practice in any special difficulties of either time or tune which may arise in a lesson. It must not be assumed that every tune in these books is necessarily more difficult than those immediately preceding it. Excepting for the new factor, the first tunes in each Section are sometimes easier than those at the end of the previous Section. But the Sections are arranged in order of difficulty and the tunes graded within each Section.

Section IC introduces a quaver as a beat. Examples of a minim as a beat will be found in Book VII.

SUGGESTED PLANS FOR READING

It is suggested that each tune may be sung in all of the following ways:

1) To solfa without time.

2) In monotone (a) to time names, (b) to doh.

3) Combined time and tune to solfa.

4) Combined time and tune to laa, twice if necessary, and then once at least with all expression marks observed (and to an accompaniment where the teacher is sufficiently skilled to improvise one).

D0366188

The class should always beat time or tap each beat silently.

When the class is more advanced each test should be sung at least three times, as follows

1) To solfa.

2) To laa.

3) With all expression marks observed (and to an accompaniment where the teacher is sufficiently skilled to improvise one).

Classes must learn to think in phrases. As an aid to this, phrasing is marked in all tunes, and cases of irregular rhythmic structure are noted. Observation of these points of construction not only helps towards more intelligent reading, but also increases the interest of the lesson. All repeats should be observed: expression marks in brackets refer to the second time.

Tempo and other indications may or may not be attended to on a first reading according to the capacity of the singers, but at a later stage all indications should be observed in order that sight-singing may be linked up with musical enjoyment. There is too often a tendency to divorce sight-singing from music, and one object of this collection is to provide material which is at once musical and useful, and which will help towards making this part of the singing lesson a delight to the class.

To add interest, the nationalities of the tunes are given. Very slight alterations have been made occasionally in order to bring tunes within the limitations of a particular section; all such cases are indicated by a *.

MODAL TUNES

In these, the keynote may be ray, me, soh, or indeed any note, and the solfa names must be according to the key signature. The term modal is usually applied to systems having notes other than doh as keynote, although, in the strict sense of the term, the ordinary major scale is also a mode.

INDEX

Tunes in the minor mode may be found in all Sections; a complete list is given below.

Section I. Nos. 1–29.

Section IA, Nos. 1–17, new time division, ♩ ♩ ♩ and ♩ ♩ ♩

Section IB, Nos. 18–24, semiquaver leaps.

Section IC, Nos. 25–29, tunes with ♩ as beat.

Section II. Nos. 30–41.
Modal tunes. (See note in Preface.)

Section III. Nos. 42–63.
Less easy use of ba and se, and of chromatic notes.

Section IV. Nos. 64–76.
Modulation. (Change of key is shown, but no solfa given.)

Section V. Nos. 77–90.
Compound time, ⅝ and ⅔ rests: ♩ ♩ ♩ taafetee.

(List of tunes in the minor mode: Nos. 10, 11, 15, 24, 26, 27, 55–64 inclusive, 66, 68, 70, 72, 74, 80, 83, 86, 89.)

Note.—The Editors wish to express their indebtedness to Messrs. Bela Bartok and Karol Hlawiczka for kind permission to use many fine Hungarian and Polish tunes from their collections. It may be noted that in these, as well as in some other melodies, the phrasing seems unusual, but it has been dictated by the original words.

FOLK SONG SIGHT SINGING SERIES
BOOK VI

Tunes in the minor mode may be found in all Sections: a complete list of the numbers is given in the Index.

SECTION I. Nos. 1-29

Section I A. Nos. 1-17 New time divisions: and

Section I B. Nos. 18-24 Semiquaver leaps

Section I C. Nos. 25-29 Quaver as a beat

Nos. 1-5.

1. Moderato — British

2. Allegro — A 3 bar phrase to end with — Bohemian

3. Moderato 2 + 3 — Polish

4. Allegro — Hungarian

Copyright, 1933, by the Oxford University Press, London. Renewed in U.S.A. 1961.

After this number all sections may contain tunes with ♩ as beat.

SECTION II. Nos. 30-41
Modal tunes

See note in preface

SECTION III. Nos. 42-63
Less easy use of ba and se and of chromatic notes.

Chromatic notes may or may not produce modulation: in this Section the cases of the former are so short that no change of tonic is necessary.

Before singing a tune the class should discover the accidentals and give the solfa names of the leaps involved.

Nos. 42-54 Major mode

14

SECTION IV. Nos. 64–76

Modulation

In each case the change of key is shown, but classes must think out the solfa for themselves.

SECTION V. Nos. 77-90
Compound Time

New time divisions: $\frac{1}{3}$ and $\frac{2}{3}$ rests. taafetee
Nos. 77-81, rests

20